Little Pebble™

Celebrate Fall

Fall Leaves

by Erika L. Shores

CAPSTONE PRESS
a capstone imprint

Little Pebble is published by Capstone Press,
1710 Roe Crest Drive, North Mankato, Minnesota 56003
www.capstonepub.com

Library of Congress Cataloging-in-Publication Data
Shores, Erika L., 1976– author.
 Fall leaves / by Erika L. Shores.
   pages cm.—(Little pebble. Celebrate fall)
 Summary: "Simple nonfiction text and full-color photographs present leaves in fall"—Provided by the publisher.
 Audience: Ages 5–7
 Audience: K to grade 3
 Includes bibliographical references and index.
 ISBN 978-1-4914-6003-0 (library binding)—ISBN 978-1-4914-6015-3 (pbk.)—
 ISBN 978-1-4914-6027-6 (ebook pdf)
 1. Leaves—Color—Juvenile literature. 2. Autumn—Juvenile literature. I. Title.
 QK649.S56 2016
 575.5'7—dc23   2015001840

Editorial Credits
Cynthia Della-Rovere, designer; Gina Kammer and Morgan Walters, media researchers;
Katy LaVigne, production specialist

Photo Credits
Dreamstime: Serrnovik, 16, 17; Shutterstock: Alekcey, cover, Dancake, (dots on borders) throughout, Denis Vrublevski, 12, 13, exopixel, (mulit colored leaves) bottom 18, 20, Hurst Photo, 1, 2, 3, Iakov Kalinin, 11, Khabibullin Damir, 21, Madlen, (autum leaves on background) backcover and throughout, Milosz_G, 6, 7, Perati Komson, 5, SP-Photo, 15, Suzanne Tucker, 19, Tatiana Grozetskaya, 9, Triff, (colored leaves on white) backcover and throughout, Triff, (colored leaves) backcover and throughout, Valentina Razumova, (green leaves) throughout

Printed in China
032015   008832LEOF15

Table of Contents

Colorful Trees

Red, yellow, and orange
cover the forest.
Fall is here.

Leaves can change color in fall. Oak leaves change to red and brown.

Maple leaves turn
red, orange,
and yellow.

8

9

Round aspen leaves
turn gold.

Evergreen trees
do not change color.
Their needles stay green.

Falling Leaves

Fall leaves die.

They drop

to the ground.

Listen! Leaves crunch
as you walk.

Rake leaves into piles.

Then jump in!

The trees are empty.

They wait for spring.

Glossary

forest—a large area thickly covered with trees and plants; forests are also called woodlands

gold—a yellow-brown color

needle—a sharp, green leaf on an evergreen tree

rake—to gather or move using a tool with a long handle

spring—the season after winter and before summer

Read More

Felix, Rebecca. *What Happens to Leaves in Fall?* Let's Look at Fall. Ann Arbor, Mich.: Cherry Lake Pub., 2013.

Owen, Ruth. *How Do You Know It's Fall?* Signs of the Seasons. New York: Bearport Pub., 2012.

Smith, Sian. *What Can You See in Fall?* Seasons. Chicago: Capstone Heinemann Library, 2015.

Internet Sites

FactHound offers a safe, fun way to find Internet sites related to this book. All of the sites on FactHound have been researched by our staff.

Here's all you do:
Visit *www.facthound.com*
Type in this code: 9781491460030

 Check out projects, games and lots more at
www.capstonekids.com

Index